Weekend Whittling Projects

By Sara Barraclough

Contents

Introduction

I am so excited to introduce these four little carving projects! They are designed to be made with just a carving knife and some imagination—no cutouts or power tools, just good ol' fashioned whittling. There's plenty of room to add your own flair and personality once you get the general shapes down.

People who know me know that I carve in my car—A LOT. All of these creatures were created in my car, so all I had were a detail knife and a rough out knife. I like my carvings to be easily transportable, so you can carve one anywhere—from a campsite to a baseball game. Although these are "small" carves, there is plenty of material to take off, so MAKE THOSE CHIPS FLY!

One of my main goals when carving is to make the end design look nothing like the original block—so don't be afraid to make deep cuts and take off more material than you might be used to. The projects are meant to be on the "cartoony" side, with exaggerated details and features. With a few strategically placed cuts, you'll have a myriad of options for little changes and personalization. The #1 goal is to have fun (and maybe impress your friends with a cute little creature)!

Before You Begin

I get a lot of questions about painting and antiquing. As a general rule, I water down my paints substantially. It is much easier to add an extra coat of paint than it is to take paint off. Plus, I like to see some of the wood grain when it's all said and done. I usually follow approximately a 10:1 ratio (10 drops of water to every one healthy drop of acrylic paint).

I also get many questions on shading/antiquing. I liken it to the peaks and valleys of a mountain range. Mountain peaks are always in the sunlight, so they will look lighter; valleys are shady and dark. The same concept applies to carvings. In the places with deep cuts (under hat brims, arm creases, between pants and shoes, etc.), you want to apply a darker shade of antiquing wax, leaving the high spots alone. Working with the peaks and valleys will add lots of personality and depth to your finished carving.

Plucky Penguins

Carve a colony of flightless birds—with just one knife!

I came up with these silly little penguins as I was sitting in my car waiting for my daughter. We were in a "penguin everything" phase, and I wanted to make a quick gift that would bring a smile to her face. I thought a penguin with a whimsical hat would do the trick—and it did. I chose to carve these on the corner because it allows the beak to stand out a little more than usual, giving them depth and personality.

The fun thing about these little guys is that they're easily scaled up or down and have endless possibilities for hat shapes and painting patterns. You can turn them into everything from shelf sitters to ornaments and carve them from start to finish with one knife. They are delightfully quick and easy— and, needless to say, super cute! *Note: I always wear a carving glove. The photos were taken without one to clearly show hand and knife positions.*

1 **Draw the basic landmarks.** Make a horizontal line where the brim of the hat will sit, about halfway or 1.5" (3.8cm) from the top. Then draw the beak on one of the corners of the blank.

2 **Start to remove material from the hat.** Use a knife. Round all the sharp corners and taper the hat slightly toward the top, giving the blank a pear shape. Round it evenly on all sides.

3 **Shape the hat.** Create a bend about ¼" (6mm) down from the top of the blank. To do this, make a stop cut straight into the side and carve up to it in several short strokes. (Too much force will knock off the tip of the hat.) Make a stop cut around the entire base of the hat, carving up to it to separate the hat from the head.

4 **Round the sides and back of the penguin.** As you start to remove more material, you can also remove some material from the hat to keep it in proportion. Bring the body into the hat brim and round off the bottom of the piece to give him a plump, little body. Try to remove as many "flat" sides as you can while keeping the carving in proportion. DO NOT carve the nose and face yet.

5

Shape the beak. Remove wood from the top and bottom to establish the height of the face. Then make V-cuts following the line of the beak on each side, outlining the triangle.

6

Round the beak slightly. Soften the hard edge along the perimeter, but don't remove too much material—you want it to stand out from the body. *Note: It might be easier to use a smaller knife for the beak portion; I have sometimes used a 1" (25mm) detail knife. However, I have completed many of my penguins with just a 1½" (38mm) knife.*

7

Add the tuxedo lines. From the front, they should look like a small circle on top of a larger circle. Making a V-cut (keeping your blade at an angle), follow the lines with the knife to create depth between the body (which will be painted black) and the belly (which will be painted white). Clean up any fuzzies or slivers with a small square of 220-grit sandpaper, if desired.

Before You Paint

Painting preferences differ from one carver to the next. I prefer my paint to be thinner so that some of the wood grain shows through. It's easier to start with thinner paint and add layers to darken it rather than starting too dark and trying to lighten it. When in doubt, add more water to your paint than you think you'll need. I use about a 1:10 ratio (one small, pea-sized drop of paint to 10 drops of water).

PAINTING

8

Dip your penguin in boiled linseed oil. Allow the excess to drip off and wipe it down with clean paper towels. Make sure to wipe the creases and crevices to get any "pools" of oil off. The oil changes the way the wood takes the paint and can reduce bleeding of color into unwanted areas. *Note: Dispose of used paper towels according to the manufacturer's instructions on the container of oil, as oil-soaked rags can spontaneously combust.*

9 Paint the penguin.

Cover the body in watered-down black, the belly in watered-down vintage white, and the beak in orange. Paint his hat using a watered-down 2:1 ratio of Hauser dark green and light avocado, and allow it to dry before adding the dots (painting the dots before the base color dries usually results in bleeding).

10 Add the hat details.

Dip the end of a stylus or paintbrush in vintage white paint and apply clusters of dots up the surface of the hat (starting from the bottom and working your way to the top). Let dry.

11 Add the eyes.

Make two large dots for the eyes with the end of a paintbrush dipped in black. Allow to dry. Then dip the edge of a stylus in vintage white and add a smaller, white dot near the center of each eye, facing inward.

Finishing

Using a watered-down antiquing wax (3:1 ratio of water to wax), apply the mixture to the creases and wipe it away, being careful not to make the belly look "dirty." The idea is to add a little depth to the different areas but not a full-on antiqued look. When in doubt, remember that, as with paint, less is more.

Finish as desired. I prefer to seal my projects with a wax finish, such as Howard Feed-N-Wax, or spray them with a satin sealer, such as Krylon.

Penguin Patterns

materials & tools

MATERIALS
- Basswood, 1½" (3.8cm) square: main penguin, 3" (7.6cm) long
- Acrylic paint, such as Folk Art: ebony black, Hauser dark green, light avocado, tangerine, vintage white
- Pencil
- Sandpaper: 220-grit (optional)
- Boiled linseed oil
- Antiquing wax
- Finish, such as Howard Feed-N-Wax or Krylon satin spray
- Paper towels

TOOLS
- Carving knife
- Detail knife (optional)
- Stylus
- Paintbrushes: assorted small

The author used these products for the project. Substitute your choice of brands, tools, and materials as desired.

Shrimpy

We mustache you a question—how many ways can *you* carve this versatile design?

Shrimpies, as I call them, are some of my favorite characters to carve. They are small and cute and the possibilities are endless. Once you have the general shape and cuts down, you can make them into Santas, gnomes, sea captains—whatever you can come up with.

PREPPING AND CARVING

1 **Draw the guidelines for the hat.** The front brim will fall approximately a third of the way down from the top. Then angle it down around the sides so that the back of the hat lands halfway down. Make a stop cut at each of the corners and cut up toward the brim to separate the hat from the head. Use a rough out knife. Start rounding the corners and shaping the top of the hat.

2 Start to shape the nose. This is easier with a smaller blade length, so I switched to a detail knife. Separate the top of the nose from the brim of the hat and outline the bottom of the nose, making a stop cut and then carving up to it. The deeper you make these cuts, the more personality and definition your carving will have. Make the nose bigger than you think it needs to be, so you'll have material to take off in the shaping and detailing phase. Continue tapering the hat upward, leaving plenty of room for the bend at the tip.

3 Continue rounding the hat and body. Use the detail knife. Then clear more material from around the nose to make it stand out. Round the nose until it begins to look like a slightly flat oval, and pencil in the shape of the mustache.

4 Establish the mustache. There is plenty of material to remove, which will allow you to place the outer brim of the hat, the nose, the mustache, and the body all on different planes. (The nose sticks out farther than the mustache, the mustache overlaps the body, etc.) The goal is to give the shrimpy multiple 'layers' when viewed from the side. Pencil in the shoes roughly ¼" (6.4mm) up from the bottom.

5 Carve the shoes. Follow the lines you just made with extended V-cuts to separate the shoes from the robe. The deeper you make your cuts, the more dimension you give the overall look. Then draw the belt and belt buckle in the space between the mustache and feet. If the shoes or mustache are bigger than expected, you can tuck the buckle under the mustache and extend it around the body as usual.

6 Add the belt details. Make stop cuts to separate the belt from the body, and then carve up to them on the top and bottom so the belt protrudes slightly.

7 Add the mustache texture. If you have a small ¹⁄₁₆" (1.6mm) V-tool, it will make the job easier, but you can also use a regular detail knife. Make small V-cuts fanning down and out from the center of the nose. Give them a slightly random look. Then add the buckle to the front of the belt. At this point, do an overall inventory of the shrimpy to round any flat areas and add final details.

8 **Paint the clothing base coats.** For the hat, mix 2 drops of light avocado with one drop of Hauser dark dreen and about 15-20 drops of water. If it's too light for your liking, add more paint. For the robe, mix 2 drops of midnight blue with 15 drops of water. Paint in washes until you're satisfied with the colors.

9 **Paint the nose and cheeks.** Dip the tip of a paintbrush into the cap of true red, and then wipe that onto your paint pallet. Add a few drops of water—it should be an extremely watery red. Apply that to the top of the nose and the cheeks. Paint the mustache with watered-down burnt umber.

10 **Paint the belt and shoes.** I used 1 drop of bittersweet chocolate mixed with about 12 drops of water. The belt and shoes should be relatively light so as to show off the effect of the antiquing wax. Paint the buckle with slightly thinned metallic gold.

11 **Antique the carving.** Personally, I don't cover the carving in antiquing wax and then wipe it off—it tends to look too 'dirty' for my liking. Thin your antiquing wax; I mix 2 parts wax to 1 part water. Apply the wax to the underside of the hat brim, the top of the nose, the valleys above the shoes, and the point where the belt meets the robe—anywhere you have cut "in." Seal as desired; I prefer a natural finish such as Howard Feed-N-Wax.

materials & **tools**

MATERIALS
- Basswood, 1½" (3.8cm) square: 2½" (6.3cm) tall
- Acrylic paint, such as Delta Ceramcoat: burnt umber, midnight blue; such as DecoArt: bittersweet chocolate, Hauser dark green, metallic gold, true red
- Pencil
- Sandpaper: 220-grit (optional)
- Boiled linseed oil
- Antiquing wax

- Finish, such as Howard Feed-N-Wax or Krylon

TOOLS
- Knives: rough out, detail
- Micro V-tool, ⅟₁₆" (1.6mm) (optional)
- Paintbrushes: assorted small

The author used these products for the project. Substitute your choice of brands, tools, and materials as desired.

Shrimpy Patterns

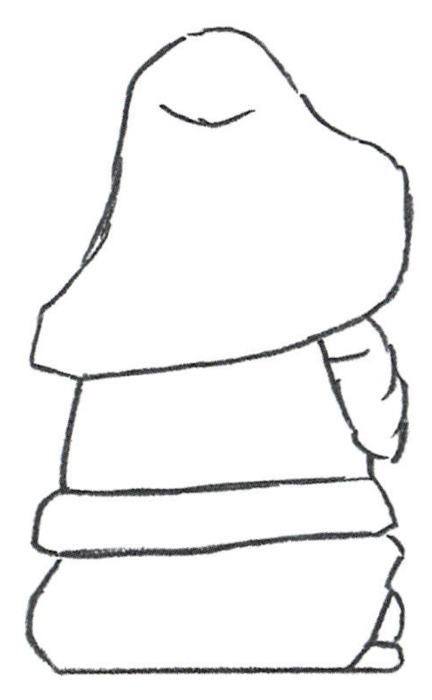

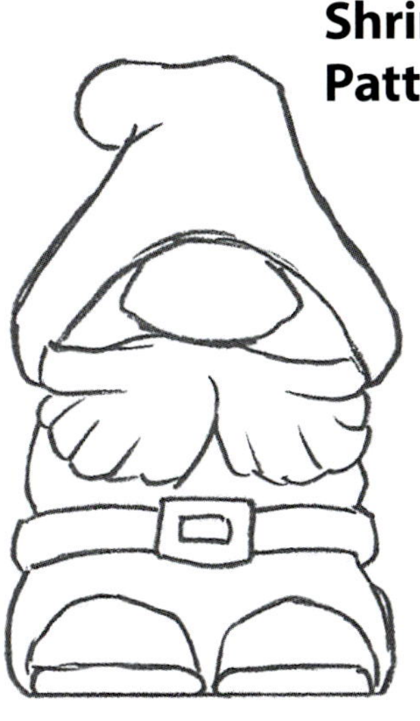

Love You Beary Much

This little bear started as a Valentine gift for my daughter. It's a quick carve and easy to paint, but is also a special way to say I love you. A few strategic cuts and attention to a couple of painting details and this stylized creature will be yours to keep—or give away!

I carved the heart balloon on the diagonal of a 12" (30.5cm) stick; because this part is smaller, it's easier to carve the majority on a longer blank so that you have something to hold onto. This is not vital—it just makes the balloon a little easier to manipulate until you get it mostly carved.

1 **Draw the basic outline.** The bear's hands will sit about halfway down, slightly below the middle of the blank

2 **Start shaping the back.** Use a detail knife. This bear has a saggy belly and a round bottom. Add a little sway in the back to provide shape (the line from the shoulders down to the bottom should look like a loose "S"). Start rounding the head, tapering it slightly from the nose area up to the crown of the head.

3 **Define the torso.** Make a stop cut along the bottom of the arms and carve up to it to give shape to the belly and separate the arms from the body. Shape the legs, cutting them back so they're overlapped by the bottom and belly.

4 **Begin shaping the face, ears, and arms.** Let the muzzle stick out slightly, and separate the ears. Define the neck area, making a deep valley where the arms meet. You can remove quite a lot of material between the muzzle and the top of the arms. Then round the arms so that the right one overlaps the left. Draw the nose.

5 **Add the nose and mouth.** Make stop cuts along the nose lines and carve up to them, going carefully so as not to snap the nose off. Round the arms and ears further. Carve the mouth, and then make a deep V-cut at the center to add interest and dimension. Narrow the head so it's slightly smaller in width than the body; the goal is to remove some of the bear's rectangular shape.

6 **Separate the legs.** Round the belly and bottom further, so they hang over his feet. Keep refining the body, rounding out any flat areas and cleaning up any untidy cuts.

7 **Drill the hole for the balloon string.** Depending on the angle of your bear, it will probably be easier to drill down about halfway from the top, and then drill halfway up from the bottom. Because the arms are so close to the body, you may find it easier to separate the wire for the balloon into two parts (top and bottom) instead of trying to drill straight through.

ADDING THE DETAILS

8 **Make the balloon.** Draw your guidelines on the diagonal (so the center of the heart falls on a corner), and establish the general shape of the heart. Tweak it according to your preference; you can make a regular round or oval-shaped balloon, if desired.

9 **Refine the balloon shape.** Round any flat areas and clean up your cuts. Once you're satisfied with the shape, separate the balloon from the blank using the knife or a scroll saw.

10 **Dip the bear and balloon in boiled linseed oil.** Remove the excess and let dry. Paint the body. Mix approximately 2 drops of coffee bean with 15-20 drops of water. The body will be a fairly light brown, but this will allow the antiquing wax to show up more dramatically. Then draw the eyes and paint them with unthinned titanium white, using a fine-tip paintbrush dipped right into the paint cap. Allow the white to dry, and paint a smaller black raindrop over the top. Let dry.

11 **Add the eyelashes.** I used a fine black permanent pen to add three or four lashes to the outer bottom corner of each eye. Once they are dry, add slightly thinned antiquing wax to all the creases of the arms, the insides of the ears, and the creases of the legs (both front and back). You can also add some to the nose to make it darker than the muzzle.

12 **Paint the balloon.** I used slightly thinned black cherry. Once it has dried, take the wire and wrap it around the bottom of the heart. You can take a pair of pliers and gently squeeze it around the balloon to secure it in place, but be careful not to damage the wire. Take a second, smaller piece of wire and secure it to the bottom with a few drops of cyanoacrylate (CA) glue, giving it a small curve. Then do the same with the upper portion of wire. Finish as desired; I prefer Howard Feed-N-Wax.

Love You Beary Much Patterns

materials & tools

MATERIALS
- Basswood, 1½" (3.8cm) square: bear, 3⅝" (9.2cm)
- Basswood, 1¼" (3.2cm) square: balloon, 1¾" (4.4cm) (or longer if desired)
- Acrylic paint, such as Folk Art: black cherry, coffee bean, pure black, titanium white
- Pencil
- Permanent pen: black, fine-tip
- Sandpaper: 220-grit (optional)
- Glue: cyanoacrylate (CA)
- Boiled linseed oil
- Antiquing wax
- Finish, such as Howard Feed-N-Wax or Krylon
- Aluminum wire, 14 gauge: 5" (12.7cm) long

TOOLS
- Detail knife
- Scroll saw (optional)
- Handheld drill with bit: 1⁄16" (1.6mm)-dia.
- Paintbrushes: assorted small, fine-tipped

The author used these products for the project. Substitute your choice of brands, tools, and materials as desired.

Shelly the Snail

Whittle a classic slowpoke with lots of personality.

Who doesn't love a cute little snail—especially of the non-slimy variety? Even though you'll have to remove a fair amount of material around her head, Shelly is a fairly simple project to complete. Once you get the shape down, there are endless ways to make little changes; soon, you'll have a whole family of snails. Play around with mixing complementary colors for the shell—get creative and don't be afraid to experiment!

PREPPING AND CARVING

1 **Trace the pattern onto the blank.** The shell will make up the majority of the blank (approximately ⅔).

2 **Establish the basic shape.** Use a rough out knife. Begin separating the shell from the head and bringing in the sides; the head and torso of the snail are fairly narrow compared to the width of the shell.

3 **Round the shell and start shaping the torso and head.** Use the same knife. Leave enough material on top of the head so you'll have room to add some nice big eyes later. Don't take too much from around the bottom, either; you'll need to leave a small ribbon of body poking out from under the shell. You'll want to leave about ¼" (6.4mm) of excess around the bottom.

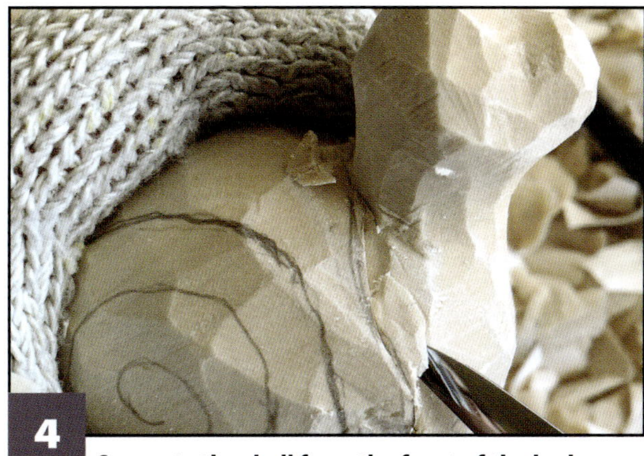

4 **Separate the shell from the front of the body.** Make a smooth stop cut along the shell line and carve up to it from the neck area. Then draw the shell swirl.

5 **Define the nose.** Then add a ridge around the shell that arcs around the front like a collar. Round the shell more thoroughly to get rid of the overly square shape.

6 **Carve the shell swirl.** The outside of the swirl should start toward the front corner and spiral counter-clockwise toward the back. Leave enough space between the swirls to give each one definition; if the swirl is too tight, you lose the crisp lines.

7 **Add the body ripple.** This is probably the most delicate part of the carving—you want to have a sharp knife, but take extra care not to split the wood. The goal is to create a 'ribbon' around the bottom to make it look like the snail is moving. Decide where you want the 'highs and lows' to go before you start carving, making them fairly even around the bottom. Use the rough out knife and then a detail knife.

8 **Detail the eyes.** Separate them from the head, keeping them big and cartoonishly round. You want them to be a part of the head but look like they are sitting on top of the nose, facing slightly forward. Use the detail knife. Lightly sand if desired, and then dip the snail in boiled linseed oil. Allow the excess to drip off and wipe it down with clean paper towels to remove any excess. *Note: Dispose of used paper towels according to the manufacturer's instructions on the container of oil, as oil-soaked rags can spontaneously combust.*

9 **Paint the body and shell base coats.** I chose purple for the shell because it goes nicely with the green, but feel free to get creative with your colors. Cover the shell in a diluted eggplant (2 drops of paint to 15-20 drops of water). You'll add a few coats, so don't worry if it seems light at first. Paint the body with a mixture of 2 drops light avocado and 1 drop pistachio; it will darken with the antiquing wax.

10 **Add some contrasting color to the shell.** I added watered-down midnight blue into the creases of the spiral and some frosted plum to the high points on the shell. The colors should blend together, but feel free to add more eggplant if you want darker purple in some areas. You can also add some watered-down antiquing wax to the valleys of the spiral, the ribbon, and front of the shell (between the shell and body).

11 **Paint the eyes.** I used slightly thinned titanium white and a fine-tip paintbrush. Add the irises and pupils. Once the white has dried, add two black dots (I just use the opposite end of my paintbrush). Once those have dried, add a small white dot near the center of each, facing inward slightly. Finish with Howard Feed-N-Wax or a natural finish of your choice.

materials & **tools**

MATERIALS

- Basswood, 2" (5.1cm) square: 3¼" (8.3cm)
- Acrylic paint, such as DecoArt: frosted plum, light avocado; such as Folk Art: eggplant, midnight, pistachio, pure black, titanium white
- Pencil
- Sandpaper: 220-grit (optional)
- Boiled linseed oil
- Antiquing wax
- Finish, such as Howard Feed-N-Wax or Krylon

The author used these products for the project. Substitute your choice of brands, tools, and materials as desired.

TOOLS

- Knives: rough out, detail
- Paintbrushes: fine tip, assorted small

Shelly the Snail Patterns

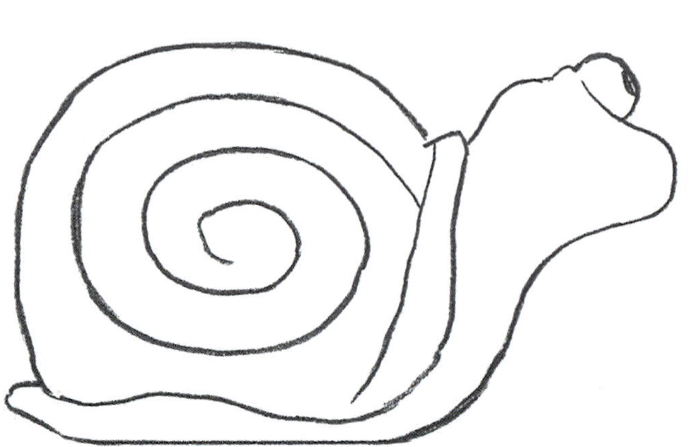